ANTHONY EDWARDS

BY BO MITCHELL

Apex is distributed by North Star Editions:
sales@northstareditions.com | 888-417-0195

Produced for Apex by Red Line Editorial.

Photographs ©: Marta Lavandier/AP Images, cover; Rick Scuteri/AP Images, 1, 20–21; David Zalubowski/AP Images, 4–5; Kyusung Gong/AP Images, 6; Shutterstock Images, 8, 10–11, 12, 13, 16–17; Craig Lassig/AP Images, 9, 29; Mark Humphrey/AP Images, 15; Thomas Shea/Pool USA Today Sports/AP Images, 18–19; Darren Abate/AP Images, 22–23; Andy Clayton-King/AP Images, 24–25; Brandon Dill/AP Images, 26

Library of Congress Control Number: 2022923267

ISBN
978-1-63738-554-8 (hardcover)
978-1-63738-608-8 (paperback)
978-1-63738-712-2 (ebook pdf)
978-1-63738-662-0 (hosted ebook)

Printed in the United States of America
Mankato, MN
082023

NOTE TO PARENTS AND EDUCATORS

Apex books are designed to build literacy skills in striving readers. Exciting, high-interest content attracts and holds readers' attention. The text is carefully leveled to allow students to achieve success quickly. Additional features, such as bolded glossary words for difficult terms, help build comprehension.

TABLE OF CONTENTS

CHAPTER 1

SHOOTING STAR

The Minnesota Timberwolves are facing the Denver Nuggets. It's the fourth **quarter**. The Timberwolves need to hold on to the lead.

The Minnesota Timberwolves played the Denver Nuggets on December 15, 2021.

Anthony Edwards crosses the half-court line. The Timberwolves' **point guard** passes to Edwards. Edwards takes a long shot.

FAST FACT

Edwards usually plays shooting guard. Players in this position focus on making long shots.

Anthony Edwards made 215 three-pointers in the 2021–22 season.

A three-pointer is a shot made from behind the three-point line on the court's floor.

Swish! The ball drops through the net. It's Edwards's 10th three-pointer of the game. His teammates cheer. The Timberwolves win 124–107.

RECORD BREAKER

Edwards set two records against the Nuggets. He became the youngest NBA player to make 10 three-point shots in one game. He also became the youngest Timberwolves player to score 2,000 career points.

Fans love to watch Edwards make exciting plays.

CHAPTER 2

EARLY LIFE

Anthony Edwards was born in Atlanta, Georgia. He loved football as a kid. But he decided to focus on basketball in high school. He worked hard to become a good shooter.

Atlanta is the largest city in Georgia. It's also the state's capital.

The University of Georgia's basketball team plays at Stegeman Coliseum in Athens, Georgia.

Anthony's hard work paid off. He became one of the top high school players in the country. In college, he played basketball for the University of Georgia.

The University of Georgia's mascot is a bulldog named Uga.

Edwards played well in college, too. But his team struggled. Georgia won only half of its games.

COLLEGE STAR

Edwards averaged 19.1 points per game during his first season at Georgia. He led all college **freshmen** in scoring. And he was named the Southeastern **Conference** Freshman of the Year.

Edwards jumps to dunk the ball during a 2020 game against Vanderbilt.

CHAPTER 3

GOING PRO

After one year of college, Edwards decided he was ready for the NBA. The Minnesota Timberwolves chose him in the NBA **Draft**. He was the first overall pick.

The Timberwolves play at Target Center in Minneapolis, Minnesota.

Edward reaches toward the basket for a dunk.

Edwards played well in his first NBA season. He finished second in Rookie of the Year voting. Fans loved his exciting **dunks**.

FAST FACT

In college, Edwards wore the number 5. He switched to the number 1 with Minnesota.

However, the Timberwolves struggled during Edwards's rookie season. They went 23–49 and missed the **playoffs**.

HIGH SCORER

Edwards scored 42 points against the Phoenix Suns on March 18, 2021. He was 19 years old. Only two players in NBA history had ever scored 40 or more at a younger age.

Edwards drives to the hoop for a layup against the Phoenix Suns.

CHAPTER 4

YOUNG SUPERSTAR

Edwards scored even more points in his second season. He also made more of his shots. He led the Timberwolves to the **Play-In Tournament**.

Edwards averaged 21.3 points per game during the 2021–22 season.

The Timberwolves had to beat the Los Angeles Clippers to reach the playoffs. Edwards was ready. He scored 30 points, and his team won 109–104.

Edwards dunks over a Clippers defender in the fourth quarter of the play-in game.

FAST FACT

Edwards acted in a movie in 2022. He played a basketball player.

The Timberwolves faced the Memphis Grizzlies in the first round of the playoffs. The Timberwolves lost. But fans hoped for more great seasons.

PLAYOFF PRO

Edwards shined during the 2022 playoffs. He scored 36 points in the first game. Only three players had ever scored more in their first playoff game.

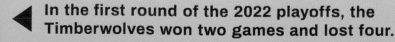

In the first round of the 2022 playoffs, the Timberwolves won two games and lost four.

COMPREHENSION QUESTIONS

Write your answers on a separate piece of paper.

1. Write a few sentences describing the main ideas of Chapter 3.

2. Which of Edwards's records do you think is most impressive? Why?

3. Which NBA team drafted Anthony Edwards?

    A. Phoenix Suns

    B. Minnesota Timberwolves

    C. Memphis Grizzlies

4. Why would setting records at a young age be harder?

    A. Young players often have better skills.

    B. Young players don't know what records are.

    C. Young players haven't played as many games.

5. What does **struggled** mean in this book?

*But his team **struggled**. Georgia won only half of its games.*

    A. had lots of success
    B. faced problems
    C. did not play games

6. What does **rookie** mean in this book?

*Edwards played well in his first NBA season. He finished second in **Rookie** of the Year voting.*

    A. a player in their first season in a league
    B. a player who scores very few points
    C. a player who listens to their coach

Answer key on page 32.

GLOSSARY

conference
A smaller group of teams within a sports league.

draft
A system where professional teams choose new players.

dunks
Baskets made by jumping up and slamming the ball through the hoop.

freshmen
Students in their first year of college.

Play-In Tournament
A set of games played after the regular NBA season to decide the final teams to make the playoffs.

playoffs
A set of games played after the regular season to decide which team will be the champion.

point guard
A position that involves running the offense and passing.

quarter
One of four parts a game is divided into.

TO LEARN MORE

BOOKS

Howell, Brian. *Minnesota Timberwolves*. Minneapolis: Abdo
Publishing, 2022.

Lilley, Matt. *The NBA Finals*. Mendota Heights, MN: Apex
Editions, 2023.

Morey, Allan. *The NBA Finals*. Minneapolis: Bellwether
Media, Inc, 2019.

ONLINE RESOURCES

Visit **www.apexeditions.com** to find links and resources
related to this title.

ABOUT THE AUTHOR

Bo Mitchell has been writing about sports since the 1990s.
He enjoys exercise, music, and having fun with his dog,
Rocky. Bo has lived in Minnesota his entire life. He's watched
a lot of Minnesota Timberwolves games.

INDEX

ANSWER KEY:
1. Answers will vary; 2. Answers will vary; 3. B; 4. C; 5. B; 6. A